LoveMORE

Marta E. Greenman

and

Maureen H. Maldonado

© 2023 Marta E. Greenman and Maureen H. Maldonado

Published by Words of Grace & Truth PO Box 860223 Plano, TX 75086.

(469) 854-3574

Words of Grace & Truth is honored to present this title in partnership with the authors. The views expressed or implied in this work are those of the authors. Words of Grace & Truth provides our imprint seal representing design excellence, creative content, and high-quality production.

No part of this publication may be reproduced, stored in a retrieval system, or transmitted in any way by any
means—electronic, mechanical, photocopy, recording, or otherwise—without the prior permission of the copyright
holder, except as provided by USA copyright law.

The authors have permission to use all the versions noted in LoveMORE: Your 30-Day Devotional in Learning to
Love Like Jesus

Scripture quotations are taken from the New American Standard Bible © Copyright 1960, 1962, 1963, 1968, 1971,
1972, 1973, 1975, 1977, 1995, 2020 by The Lockman Foundation. Used by permission.

ISBN Softcover Color: 978-1-960575-00-5
ISBN Hardcover: 978-1-960575-01-2
ISBN Softcover B&W: 978-1-960575-03-6
ISBN ePub: 978-1-960575-02-9
ISBN Mobi: 978-1-960575-04-3
ISBN Audio Book: 978-1-960575-05-0
Library of Congress Catalog Number: 2023904857

ACKNOWLEDGMENTS

To my mom, Lillie, who taught me by example to love big.

Dianne, thank you for all your labor of love in this project.

To Marshall, you always support me in the work of the Lord.

To my Lord and Savior, thank You for loving me.

Marta E. Greenman

To my parents, who taught me to love no matter what!

To Ray, for your continued support on this journey.

To Heidi, Hayley, Cody, Dustin, Eliza, Carlee, Maggie, and Collins Grace for revealing layers of love beyond my imagination.

To Jesus, thank you for being THE example of love.

Maureen H. Maldonado

Photo Credits

August Magnolia Photography (Kassandra), Allison Dunks, Cody and Carlee Ogg, Dustin and Maggie Wehunt, Kimber Boyer, Mason and Addy Wood,

FORWARD

It is unusual in this culture to find people driven to find the original meaning of the Biblical text. Yet that is what you repeatedly see in the LoveMORE Devotional. LoveMORE starts with one of the primary rules of Biblical interpretation: the Bible can never mean what it never meant. Marta and Maureen take the word and illustrate it through their real-life experiences, focusing on the lessons learned. You will find scripture passages and stories that meet you where you are in your spiritual journey. I have enjoyed this writing team; they invite you into their lives and let you see God's truth and grace.

I believe LoveMORE will touch your heart and help you love more.

Dr. Timothy W. Eaton
Christ Follower, Husband, Dad, Pastor, and Christian Educator
President of the Transnational Association of Christian Colleges and Schools,
Forest, Virginia

CONTENTS

Introducing Marta and Maureen XI

Authors' Note XV

Section One: Old Testament

Our Story - Love Comes in Many Forms 2

'Ahābâ 8

Day One – Seal of Love – Song of Solomon 8:6 12

Ahab 16

Day Two - Love is Obedience - Genesis 22:2 20

Day Three - God's Love Brings Great Power - Deuteronomy 4:37-38 24

Day Four - Covenant Love – Deuteronomy 7:9 28

My Story – Collins Grace 32

Day Five - How Will You be Remembered – Nehemiah 13:26 36

Day Six – It's Worth It – Job 19:19 40

Hesed 44

Day Seven – God Intervenes – Genesis 32:9-10 46

My Story – Neither Will I 50

Day Eight – God's Lovingkindness – Psalm 36:7 52

Day Nine – Winter – Psalm 59:16 56

Day Ten – Desert Praises – Psalm 63:3 60

Day Eleven – Folly - Psalm 85:7-8 64

My Story – Unlovable 68

Ráah 72

Day Twelve - A Shepherd's Love – 1 Samuel 16:11 74

Yādîd 78

Day Thirteen - Lovely Dwelling Places - Psalm 84:1-2 80

Rāham 84

Day Fourteen - Gracious Compassionate Love – Isaiah 30:18 86

Section Two: New Testament

Agápé 92

Our Story - My TP Friend 96

Day Fifteen – Jesus' Love – Matthew 5:44 100

Day Sixteen - Purest Love – John 3:16 104

Day Seventeen – Follow the Commandments – John 14:21 108

Day Eighteen - Greater Love - John 15:13 112

Day Nineteen – God Demonstrated His Love – Romans 5:8 116

My Story: Angels Among Us 120

Day Twenty - Suffering Love – Romans 8:28 122

Day Twenty-one – Love Never Fails – 1 Corinthians 13:8 126

Day Twenty-two – Faith in Love – Galatians 5:6 130

Day Twenty-three – Love During Trials – 1 Thessalonians 3:12 134

Day Twenty-four – Be Ready – 2 Thessalonians 3:5 138

My Story - John's Miracle 142

Day Twenty-five – Spirit within – 2 Timothy 1:7 146

Day Twenty-six - God First Loved Us – 1 John 3:16 150

My Story - Loving Like Jesus 154

Day Twenty-seven – The Love of Jesus – Revelation 3:19 158

Day Twenty-eight – Love as the Father Loves – 1 John 2:15-16 162

Day Twenty-nine – Eternal Love – Revelation 12:11 166

Philia 170

Day Thirty - Agápé vs. Philia - John 21:17 172

Your Story 176

INTRODUCING
MARTA AND MAUREEN

Marta E Greenman

Marta left corporate America in 1998 to become a staff missionary with a church-planting organization known today as e3Partners. She led American churches in planting new ones with international church partners. During this period, Marta spent much of her time in the field on evangelism and discipleship, traveling to Colombia, Mexico, Moldova, Peru, Romania, Ukraine, Venezuela, and Zimbabwe. She also had the privilege of leading women's conferences in biblical training.

Marta began teaching inductive Bible studies in 1997 at her home church, where she taught faithfully for fifteen years. Debbie Stuart, a women's ministry director, said, "Marta Greenman is a master teacher, weaving biblical principles, personal stories, and clear application with every lesson. She walks in truth, loves the Word, and has dedicated her life to teaching that truth to women."

After seven years on the mission field in Romania, Marta began to write Bible study curriculum. Her first study, Bound to Be Free, was published in 2011. Marta founded Words of Grace & Truth in May 2011, a ministry devoted to teaching God's Word to the nations and teaching others to do the same, using the curriculum God birthed through her teaching ministry.

Leaders, Nations, God, and ACTs420NOW have been published since then. Her fourth book is a thirty-day devotional, FearLESS: God is calling you to be fearless and to fear less, co-authored with Maureen Maldonado. LoveMORE will be the second devotional co-authored with Maureen.

Marta's latest ministry venture is GraceAndTruthRadio.World (GTRW), a global radio station outreach with God's message of grace and truth. Her program, Under God, with co-host Maureen Maldonado, airs on GTRW Mondays at 3:30 p.m. CST. Marta's passion, regardless of the nation where she may be, is teaching God's Word and equipping others to lead. She is a gifted teacher, speaker, and expositor of God's Word. Marta lives in the Dallas–Fort Worth area of Texas with her husband of almost thirty years.

Maureen H Maldonado

Maureen is the second of seven children. Growing up in a home where worldly wealth was a foreign concept, she always felt treasured by her parents and knew she was rich in love. Maureen married young and raised two amazing daughters. Her grandchildren are a blessing beyond anything she could imagine. Recently, she was able to add two granddaughters-in-love who add joy to the mix; and the best yet, God has blessed her with a great-granddaughter!

Maureen has a master's degree in education from California State University and spent her career as a teacher, vice-principal, and principal in elementary education. Maureen never planned to leave California or the education system, but God had other plans.

After Maureen's husband was transferred to Arizona in 2006 and then to Texas in 2011, she spent several years teaching Just Moved, a Christian-based ministry program developed by Susan Miller for women moving homes because of life changes (https://justmoved.org). God used her teaching education and experience as a training ground to begin preparing for Him.

Involved in Bible studies in California, Arizona, and Texas, Maureen grew exponentially in her faith, love of God, and His Word. The culmination of these experiences led her to co-host the radio program Under God on GraceAndTruthRadio.World, where God's Word is taught to the nations.

Today Maureen is using her new-to-her method of studying the Bible and her long-applied teaching methods to teach the next generation of believers. Her prayer is for others to gain as much insight into God's transformational Word as she has received. She describes it as "opening the shades and letting in all the sunlight on a gloomy day." Maureen feels honored and humbled to be a part of Words of Grace & Truth and asks others to join in prayer for this needed ministry, the church, our country, and our world. LoveMORE is the second devotional Maureen has co-authored with Marta. Their first devotional was FearLESS: God is calling you to be fearless and to fear less.

Maureen and her husband, Raymond, reside in Texas, where they have transplanted almost their entire family from California.

AUTHORS' NOTE

Dear Reader,

W.A. Criswell said, "Love does not divide. It only multiplies." Today's world seems to divide everyone. The good news is that we have plenty of opportunities to love! As believers in Jesus Christ, we need to LoveMORE.

Over the next 30 days, we will examine how Jesus loved and taught His disciples to love. Jesus taught us to love our neighbors and our enemies. Learning to love as Jesus is not for the faint of heart, nor is it easy at times. But spending time each day to open our hearts to love as Jesus will set us apart from the world and prayerfully draw others to Him.

We have divided this devotional into the Old and New Testament references and different Hebrew and Greek words. Some definitions, you will notice, have a stark difference in meaning, while others are similar. Discovering the difference between earthly love versus how the Lord loves is essential to a growing relationship with Him.

Our thirty-day devotional will focus mainly on the emotion and commandment of love and its different meanings. We believe the more you love God, the more you will be able to love as God loves. Our prayer is when people see our lives, they will see a reflection of our heavenly Father. We pray your love for God and others will grow daily as you draw closer Him. We hope each day of this devotional leads you to LoveMORE.

Consumed by His Call,

Maureen & Marta

SECTION ONE:
OLD TESTAMENT

LOVE COMES IN MANY FORMS
OUR STORY: PART ONE

*T*he word "love" is often misused. We say, "I love this hamburger," or "I love your shoes."

This is not the type of love Jesus referred to in His words in John 15:9, "Just as the father has loved Me, I have also loved you; abide in My love."

Webster's dictionary describes "abide" as "to remain stable in a particular state." That does not express the love of food or clothing but God's love for humanity and one person's love for another. I realize, however, that love comes in many shapes, sizes, forms, and manners.

Marta would tell you I love people, and she is right. I am happiest when surrounded by my family and friends and feel blessed when this happens, usually around the holidays. Marta has an amazing habit of showing her love to me through chocolate pecan pies! She has been known to show up at my door with a pie in hand, and I usually try to eat my fair share.

I was quite ill with Covid a couple of years ago. Marta kept my husband and I stocked with good food. She delivered spaghetti and Romanian stew to my door. Her chicken pot pie has made its way to my table many times and is delicious. Some people have said she should bottle my spaghetti sauce.

Marta's idea of showing love is to do it through a generous heart by cooking and giving.

Maybe Marta's cooking gifts are meaningful because they remind me of my mother's love. My mom went to heaven in 1999. Her favorite method of showing love was to feed people too. She took cookies to friends and would bake pineapple upside-down cake to share with coworkers. My  children loved it when Grandma came to visit. She would go to the local market and buy crab legs (something I never splurged on as they were costly) and cook them just for my two daughters. They still talk about Grandma and her crab legs.

Food is not the only way to minister love to others. I work out regularly with my trainer, Scott. Scott is a charming young man who loves the Lord and his family. He truly enjoys working with people to increase their strength and stability. His manner of showing love is to give us an extra set of lunges or add additional weight to a pull-down bar. Nothing makes him smile more than to hear his clients tell him they thought of him every time they took a step because they were sore from a prior workout! He says he is just showing us his love!

OUR STORY: PART TWO

As an adult, I look at my mother in amazement and think about her ability to allow me to take over the kitchen as a child.

I would bake cookies or some other specialty with a childhood friend, flour would be all over the kitchen when my mother came home. She never reprimanded me. She would lovingly begin to clean up my mess and ask me about my food-making adventure.

Her generous, non-condemning spirit gave me a love for cooking and an attitude that I could make anything. Without formal training, unless you count my grandma, Bessie, or Aunt Ruth, my skills as a chef have been praised by many. My grandmother and aunt cooked the old fashion way, and so do I.

My secrets are fresh organic produce and grass-fed beef or free-range chickens. The fresher the ingredients, the better the product. Oh! And lots of butter, real butter from grass-fed cows.

Growing up as a good Baptist, food was the center of almost everything. When something good happened, you celebrated with food. When something tragic happened, you brought comfort food. Ingrained in my soul is food is the center of everything you do. But with all my adult responsibilities, cooking has become a chore, not a passion.

Today, I cook for very few people; therefore, if you receive a meal or dessert from me, it was made with love from the innermost part of my being. When I carve out time to make something special, it brings me joy, especially when

I cook for Maureen. She is such a friend to me, and she will never know how often she has said or done the perfect thing at the ideal moment.

We should make our love known to the ones we love in small and large ways. "Dear children, let us not love with words or speech but with actions and in truth" (1 John 3:18). Whom do you need to LoveMORE?

Marta

ʾahăbâ

הָאַבְהָ

The love of husband toward wife

"The noun *'ahăbâ* describes the love of husband toward wife, as that of Jacob for Rachel (Gen 29:20). God's "love" for his people is designated by the same word (Deut 7:8; II Chr 2:11; et al.). Jonathan's affection for David is also *'ahăbâ* (I Sam 18:3; 20:17; cf. II Sam 1:26).

ʾahăbâ occurs frequently in the wisdom literature and a few times in the latter prophets. Proverbs uses the word in its most abstract form: "love covers all sins" (10:12), "better a dinner where love is" (15:17; cf. Eccl 9:1, 6). Naturally, the word is used in the Song of Solomon. It is the term for "love" in several familiar verses. "His banner over me is love" (2:4). "I am sick of love" (2:5; 5:8). "Love is strong as death" (8:6). "Many waters cannot quench love" (8:7).

Famous passages in the prophets use this word as well. "I have loved you with an everlasting love" (Jer 31:3). "I drew them … with bands of love" (Hos 11:4). "And what does the Lord require of you but to do justice and to love mercy" (Mic 6:8), lit. "the love of mercy" (ʾahăbat ḥesed)."[1]

---

[1] Robert Alden, "29 בהא‎," ed. R. Laird Harris, Gleason L. Archer Jr., and Bruce K. Waltke, Theological Wordbook of the Old Testament (Chicago: Moody Press, 1999), 14.

DAY 1

SEAL OF LOVE

*"Put me like a seal over your heart, like a seal on your arm.
For love is as strong as death."*
Song of Solomon 8:6

S ong of Solomon (also known as Song of Songs) is a unique collection of songs compiled into one poem.

It seems to depict the romantic love between a man and his beloved, with a periodic chorus of "The Daughters of Jerusalem."

"Put me like a seal over your heart, like a seal on your arm. For love is as strong as death," Song of Solomon 8:6. This verse described when the couple came from the wilderness, arm in arm. The woman spoke of having her likeness put on a signet ring as a seal. Tradition dictated the ring would have been wrapped around the arm, on the hand, or worn as a necklace. It represented security and ownership and forever would be part of the wearer. She never wanted to let her beloved go. She wanted that marriage to last forever. She said, "Love is as strong as death."

Some scholars believe the woman represents the church, the Bride of Christ, and the man represents Jesus. The moment we accept Jesus as our Lord and Savior, we desire to have a permanent place in His heart. We wish to have our personal "seal" always in His presence. Ephesians 1:13 verifies this, *"In Him, you also, after listening to the message of truth, the gospel of your salvation—having also believed, you were sealed in Him with the Holy Spirit of promise."*

"Love is as strong as death." Those words are profound and true. I pray today you feel the love of Jesus and know you are forever part of His seal.

REFLECTION

1. Picture yourself walking arm-in-arm with Jesus. How do you feel?

2. Design your personal seal, which you would like to always be in the presence of Jesus.

3. Jesus' love is as strong as death. How did He prove that to us?

ahab

Love between
human beings

"There is little variation in the basic meaning of this verb. The intensity of the meaning ranges from God's infinite affection for his people to the carnal appetites of a lazy glutton.

'āhēb frequently describes love between human beings. The love of father for son is exemplified by Abraham and Isaac (Gen 22:2) and Israel and Joseph (Gen 37:3). A slave might "love" his master and wish to indenture himself to him for the rest of his life (Ex 21:8). This is the word used in the rule "love your neighbor as yourself" (Lev 19:18). "Love" of the stranger is also incumbent on the faithful (Deut 10:19). Samson had apparently told Delilah that he "loved" her (Jud 14:16; 16:15). Ruth "loved" Naomi her mother-in-law (4:15), Elkanah "loved" his wife Hannah (I Sam 1:5), and Rebekah "loved" her son Jacob (Gen 25:28). Hiram's "love" for David illustrates international friendship or irenic politics between the two (I Kgs 3:1). Notice that nowhere is the love of children toward parents mentioned. Rather, they are to honor, revere, and obey.

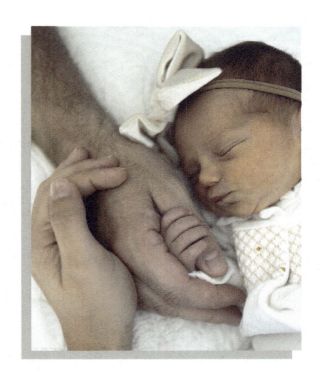

People may love things concrete or abstract. Isaac "loved" savory meat (Gen 27:4); others are said to "love" oil (Prov 21:17), silver (Eccl 5:9), and gifts (Isa 1:23). The Psalmist "loved" God's commandments (Ps 119:47). law (v. 97), testimonies (v. 119), and precepts (v. 159). Men can "love" evil (Ps 32:3 [H 5]), or death (Prov 8:36), vanity (Ps 4:2 [H 3]), cursing (Ps 109:17), or a false oath (Zech 8:17). Or they can "love" good (Amos 5:15), truth and peace (Zech 8:19), salvation (Ps 40:16 [H 17]), and wisdom (Prov 29:3).

God has commanded man to "love" him (Deut 6:5). and the Psalms contain testimonies of obedience to that commandment (116:1; 145:20). Conversely, God "loves" men, especially his people Israel (Deut 4:37; Isa 43:4; Mal 1:2). The Lord also "loves" other things, such as the gates of Zion (Ps 87:2), righteousness and judgment (Ps 33:5). and the holy temple (Mal 2:11). In a few places the verb introduces an infinitive. Jeremiah (14:10) accused the people of loving to wander, while Isaiah charged them with loving to sleep (56:10). The verb itself is sometimes an infinitive, as in Josh 22:5 and Isa 56:6. At least once it is a gerund, "a time to love" (Eccl 3:8)."[1]

---

1   Robert Alden, "29 בהא," ed. R. Laird Harris, Gleason L. Archer Jr., and Bruce K. Waltke, Theological Wordbook of the Old Testament (Chicago: Moody Press, 1999), 14.

DAY 2
LOVE IS OBEDIENCE

"He said, 'Take now your son, your only son, whom you love, Isaac, and go to the land of Moriah; and offer him there as a burnt offering on one of the mountains of which I will tell you.'"
Genesis 22:2

In God's kingdom, love is sacrifice; love is obedience.

Abraham proved his love to the King of kings by his obedience in Genesis 22.

Most are familiar with this episode. As you know, Abraham was tested by the Lord when he was directed to sacrifice his son, Isaac, as a burnt offering.

Genesis 22:1 informs us this exercise was a test. The Lord did not intend for Abraham to offer his son as a sacrifice. Hebrews 11:19 reveals Abraham believed God was able to raise men from the dead. Thus, Abraham's obedience would not have jeopardized his son.

Hebrew is the original language of the Old Testament. The words ahab (love), shachah (worship), and shama' (obey) are used together for the first time in

Genesis 22. What does this moving chapter teach us? First, Abraham's act proved that his love for God was great. Second, Abraham's obedience was a display of worship of his Lord. Third, the Hebrew word worship, šāḥâ, means to bring low, giving an indication of one humbling oneself.
In this context, Abraham was humbling himself before the Almighty God.

What was the result of Abraham's obedience? "And in your seed all the nations of the earth shall be blessed" (Genesis 22:18). Then we are told why "because you have obeyed My voice." Therefore, if we love the Lord, we will obey Him; and our obedience is an act of worshiping the Lord.

We, God's people, like Abraham, must make a choice. When we place what is most precious to us on God's altar, we obey the Lord and humble ourselves to the will of the Lord. And as Abraham, we will receive His blessing, not for the entire world, but for ourselves and those we know.

REFLECTION

1. Has God ever asked you to sacrifice something (time, money, talent) for Him? What was the known outcome?

2. Were you confident in following His command to make the sacrifice?

3. What is God asking you now to put on the altar of sacrifice?

DAY 3
GOD'S LOVE BRINGS GREAT POWER

"Because He [God] loved your fathers, therefore He chose their descendants after them. And He personally brought you from Egypt by His great power; driving out from before you nations greater and mightier than you, to bring you in and to give you their land for an inheritance, as it is today."
Deuteronomy 4:37-38

Unbelief caused the children of Israel to wander for forty years.

Except for Joshua and Caleb, their unbelief caused everyone over the age of 20 to die in the wilderness. Deuteronomy is Moses' recounting of the words the Lord had expressed forty years earlier when he met with God on Mt. Sinai.

As Deuteronomy begins, the Israelites were finally preparing to enter the Promised Land.

Most of Moses' audience had not heard his exhortation on Mt Sinai because they had not been born! It is interesting that the Hebrew word love, áhab, is used nineteen times in Deuteronomy; yet the book is known as the Second Law.

Deuteronomy 4:37-38 advised the next generation, "Because He [God] loved your fathers, therefore He chose their descendants after them. And He personally brought you from Egypt by His great power; driving out from before you nations greater and mightier than you, to bring you in and to give you their land for an inheritance, as it is today." God's love always multiplies. Why did the next generation receive the Lord's gracious hand? The Lord was gracious to them because He loved their fathers, the previous generation.

Moses wanted to ensure the Israelites understood how greatly the Lord loved His people and the great lengths to which He would go to prove His love.

Today, there is a generation that does not know God, who He is, or how much He loves them! We must become like Moses, Joshua, and Caleb so we can tell all that the Lord has done because He loves us. The next generation must understand the words Moses taught in Deuteronomy 4:39, "Know therefore today, and take it to your heart, that the Lord, He is God in heaven above and on the earth below; there is no other."

REFLECTION

1. How did the Lord bring you out of your Egypt?

2. How did He drive out nations greater and mightier than you?

3. What land has He given you?

DAY 4
COVENANT LOVE

"Know therefore that the Lord your God, He is God, the faithful God, who keeps His covenant and His lovingkindness to a thousandth generation with those who love Him and keep His commandments."
Deuteronomy 7:9

Why do we often seem to focus on the negative instead of the positive?

As a child, I remember hearing of God cursing sin even to the third and fourth generation (Exodus 34:7). Yet I was a Christian many years before I heard anyone speak on Deuteronomy 7:9, which tells of the Lord keeping covenant to a thousand generations! God kept a kingdom for David's descendants on the throne of Israel even after Solomon forsook the Lord.

The Lord keeping covenant for a thousand generations is exciting! What does this verse teach? It tells us the Lord is faithful; we can depend upon Him, unlike the world around us. We learn that God is a covenant God. What does this mean? This means we can trust God to do as He promised. Covenant is a binding agreement. In Biblical times, the covenant was not ratified until the person initiating the covenant died. As with a last will and testament, until the originator dies, his intentions are not executed.

In Genesis 15, God cut a covenant with Abram (Abraham); however, this called for the death of God to secure the Covenant. This was accomplished 2,000 years later when God sent Jesus to His sacrificial death on the cross to pay for the sins of humanity, thus blessing the thousands of generations who love Him and keep His commandments. I often say obedience always equals blessings. Yes, in God's lovingkindness, He chooses to bless us to a thousandth generation through His Son, Jesus. We don't deserve it; we can earn it, but we must receive it. "For God so loved the world, that He gave His only begotten Son, that whoever believes in Him shall not perish, but have eternal life" (John 3:16).

REFLECTION

1. Have you ever made a solemn promise? Describe it.

2. Has anyone ever broken a promise they made to you? How did it affect you?

3. Name a time you felt God's promise to love you.

MY STORY
COLLINS GRACE

As I write this story, my eyes are full of happy tears, and my heart is truly about to explode with pure joy and thankfulness.

You see, my great-granddaughter was just born to my grandson, who stole my heart from the moment I saw him on ultrasound 30 years ago, and his sweet loving wife.

This is a great story of love, faithfulness, trust, and, most of all, God's goodness.

During the summer of 1992, Southern California was struck by two very serious earthquakes in the early morning hours of June 28. Severe damage was felt throughout the town where I lived. It was an unsettling time as we were in constant fear of aftershocks or another quake.

Three days later, I received my own personal "earthquake". My seventeen-year-old daughter, Hayley (who had never given me one moment of trouble), and her then ex-boyfriend came to my office to tell me she was pregnant. I felt as if the world just froze in time, then as if it were spinning, and then as if it would never stop shaking. Buildings did not crumble, and glass did not break, but my hopes, dreams, and plans for my child were in a heap beneath the rubble. Yes, I think I went a little crazy for the next few days and tried to figure out a solution to this huge "problem".

Shame, embarrassment, anger, sadness, foolishness, and shock are just some of the feelings I remember. Abortion was never an option in our home. We would raise the child in our home, and Hayley would complete high school. We would make the best of a difficult situation.

I was still a mom, however, and went with my daughter to doctor appointments and cared for her as needed. I will NEVER forget the day of her first ultrasound. She was 7 months into her pregnancy, and I accompanied her to an ultrasound. Trust me, I was still not thrilled about this baby but kept praying God would intervene …. somehow.

God has never failed me. That day, during the ultrasound procedure, that baby in the womb looked directly at me and stole my heart.

Cody was my first grandchild. He was born on January 12, 1993, and has been a joy to everyone who has ever known him. I describe this grandparent thing as though we are an onion. A new layer is peeled off, and a whole new level of love comes out when you have a grandchild.

My daughter, Hayley, also grew up and blossomed through all this and has been a wonderful parent. I never stopped praying for my grandson Cody, and he was on my prayer list weekly in my group studies while he was in high school and college. We prayed God would protect him and grow in his love for Jesus, and God would bring him a Jesus-loving wife.

All these things have happened!!!! Cody loves the Lord with all his heart, and his wife, Carlee, does as well. Now, they have peeled back another layer of my love and brought forth a beautiful baby girl, Collins Grace. You see, God's love never divides; it only multiplies.

"And as for you, you meant evil against me, but God meant it for good" (Genesis 50:20). He has proven this to me over and over in my life, but Collins is the icing on the cake! Matthew 24:12-13, "…most people's love will grow cold. But the one who endures to the end, he shall be saved."

We have all endured, and we shall all be saved. I know deep in my heart and soul that Jesus loves me. My humanity does not allow me to grasp the true depth of that love, but if it's even one small percent of my love for my new great-granddaughter, then I cannot wait to meet Jesus and be wrapped in His arms.

DAY 5
HOW WILL YOU BE REMEMBERED?

"Did not Solomon king of Israel sin regarding these things? Yet among the many nations there was no king like him, and he was loved by his God, and God made him king over all Israel; nevertheless the foreign women caused even him to sin."
Nehemiah 13:26

On his deathbed, David passed the kingdom to Solomon. He encouraged Solomon to walk in God's ways and keep His statutes and commandments.

Not only would Solomon have success, but also David and his descendants would continue to hold the throne of Israel (1 Kings 2:1-4).

Solomon prayed for wisdom; God not only granted him wisdom but also great wealth. Of all Nehemiah could have said about Solomon, he named Solomon's sin and compared it with an existing situation in Jerusalem.

Nehemiah called out the leaders of Jerusalem for marrying and allowing their children to marry foreign women who enticed them to worship unknown gods. Despite that blatant defiance, Nehemiah wanted them to know God chose to love Solomon and used him mightily in Israel's history. So, since God loved Solomon, God also loved them.

What is the application for us? First, God wants an intimate relationship with us, but sin separates us from Him by interfering with our bond and our communication. God loves us so much that He will NOT allow us to stay in

that sinful condition. Second, our failures do not disqualify us from serving our King.

2,000 years ago, God sent His only Son, Jesus, to pay the penalty for our sins. When we accept His redemptive salvation, Jesus washes our sins away. God's love puts us into His service for the kingdom of God.

REFLECTION

1. Has your sin separated you from God? What was the circumstance and result?

2. What steps do you need to take to restore the relationship?

3. Write a prayer to God asking for forgiveness and seeking His perfect love.

DAY 6
IT'S WORTH IT

*"All my associates abhor me,
And those I love have turned against me."
Job 19:19*

The book of Job is one of my favorites and one of my least favorite of the Bible.

The man, Job, is described as "blameless, upright, fearing God, and turning away from evil" Job 1:1. Yet, God allowed Satan to bring unspeakable calamity upon him and all he loved. This book is about pain and a deeper relationship with God. I have studied this book of the Bible intently, once with a group of Bible scholars, yet writing this devotional, I realized one of the reasons God allowed Job to suffer was to bring him into an even deeper relationship with Himself.

1 Thessalonians 5:18 says, «in everything give thanks; for this is God's will for you in Christ, Jesus." This is one of the most challenging commands. Job is the ultimate example of proving his love for the Lord in truly horrendous circumstances.

Job seemed to be full of anguish, "All my associates abhor me, and those I love have turned against me," Job 19:19. He lamented that his best friends, those with whom he had shared his deepest secrets,  detested him, and the people he loved had turned against him. Those were his favorite people in the world.

God showed His love and care for Job by redeeming him. Job 42:7 tells us, "It came about after the Lord had spoken these words to Job, that the Lord said to Eliphaz the Temanite, "My wrath is kindled against you and against your two friends because you have not spoken of Me what is right as My servant Job has."

I wonder, did Job understand real love only comes from our Creator? Was the Lord allowing him to suffer so Job would finally know God's true, never-ending love?

REFLECTION

1. What is God allowing (or has allowed) to draw you closer to Him?

2. Did you grow closer to God through the circumstance? How?

3. Are you prepared to let go of all your earthly loves to realize the full love of Jehovah?

ḥesed

חֶסֶד

Mercy, kindness, love

"For centuries the word ḥesed was translated with words like mercy, kindness, love.

In 1927 Nelson Glueck, shortly preceded by I. Elbogen, published a doctoral dissertation in German translated into English by A. Gottschalk, Hesed in the Bible with an introduction by G. A. LaRue which is a watershed in the discussion. His views have been widely accepted. In brief, Glueck built on the growing idea that Israel was bound to its deity by covenants like the Hittite and other treaties. He held that God is pictured as dealing basically in this way with Israel. The Ten Commandments, etc. were stipulations of the covenant, Israel's victories were rewards of covenant keeping, her apostasy was covenant violation and God's hesed was not basically mercy, but loyalty to his covenant obligations, a loyalty which the Israelites should also show. He was followed substantially by W. F. Lofthouse (1933), N. H. Snaith (1944), H. W. Robinson (1946), Ugo Masing (1954), and many others.

There were others, however, who disagreed. F. Assension (1949) argued for mercy, basing his views on the ot versions. H. J. Stoebe (doctoral dissertation 1951, also articles in 1952 VT and in THAT) argued for good-heartedness, kindness. Sidney Hills and also Katherine D. Sakenfeld (The Meaning of Ḥesed in the Hebrew Bible, a New Inquiry), held in general that ḥesed denotes free acts of rescue or deliverance which in prophetic usage includes faithfulness. For this historical survey and references see Sakenfeld pp. 1–13 (hereafter called Sak.); also LaRue in the book by Glueck (here called G.)"[1]

---

1 R. Laird Harris, "698 חסד," ed. R. Laird Harris, Gleason L. Archer Jr., and Bruce K. Waltke, *Theological Wordbook of the Old Testament* (Chicago: Moody Press, 1999), 305.

DAY 7
GOD INTERVENES

*"I am unworthy of all the lovingkindness and of all the faithfulness
which Thou has shown to Thy servant; for with my staff only I crossed this Jordan, and now I have become two companies."
Genesis 32:10*

We first met Jacob in Genesis 25.

He was a twin son of Isaac and Rebecca and the grandson of Abraham. At his birth, he was described as "his hand holding on to Esau's heel" Genesis
26:26. Throughout his young life, Jacob seemed to have made questionable decisions that eventually caused him to flee his native country.

Chapter 29 brings Jacob to the land of his relative, Laban. Laban had a beautiful daughter, Rachel, with whom Jacob fell instantly in love. Laban had other plans, however, and it is quite a story. I encourage you to pick up your Bible and read the account of Jacob and Laban, Genesis 28:5-Genesis 32. You won't be able to stop reading!

Laban was Jacob's employer for 20 years, and had changed his contract several times. God intervened when Laban tried to cheat Jacob, proving His "lovingkindness." Jacob wanted to move his family to his homeland. Jacob eventually fled from his father-in-law with his wives, children, livestock, and all their possessions. Laban tried to stop them in Genesis 30:27, "But Laban said to him, 'If I have found favor in your eyes, please stay. …The Lord has blessed me because of you." Laban was looking after his own best interests!

20 years prior, Jacob had fled his birthplace with only his rod. Genesis 32 tells of him with his family on the journey to his homeland. In Genesis 32:9-10, Jacob acknowledges the lovingkindness which God had shown him all his life, "I am unworthy of all the lovingkindness and of all the faithfulness which Thou has shown to Thy servant; for with my staff only I crossed this Jordan, and now I have become two companies." Genesis 32: 9-10.

Jacob is proof that God will forgive and bless us if we turn from our wrong decisions and follow His path. God truly wants to bless His children. We always have the opportunity to turn our face toward our Father and for his "lovingkindness."

God's lovingkindness can flow through us to others or from others to us. We are told to "love like Jesus" so others may see Him. We see this love on display in a teacher taking extra time with students in need, or a nurse giving an encouraging word to a patient who has not had visitors. The world seems to be in such chaos, and I believe displays of lovingkindness are more needed now than ever.

Maureen

REFLECTION

1. How has God blessed you with His "lovingkindness" to make you more comfortable?

2. Who has shown you a particular moment of "lovingkindness"?

3. What is your plan TODAY to demonstrate God's lovingkindness to a stranger (grocery clerk, older adult, child, etc.)?

NEITHER WILL I
MY STORY

***M**arriage is not for the faint of heart. Especially when you begin a relationship as a non-believer, then God radically transforms your life.*

I became a believer first, then Marshall, my husband, followed a few years later. Unlike myself, who had been raised in a Christian home, Marshall had no reference for what a Christian or Christian marriage should look like.

As a result, our marriage began to unravel. We found ourselves in marriage counseling and felt like it was our only hope. We usually went to counseling together, but Marshall went alone on one rare occasion. I will never forget what happened. He came home angry. He got inches from my face and loudly proclaimed, "We're going to be married forever, so we better get this right!"

The next several weeks were notably better until we had then a major blowup. At the time, I was a financial advisor and had an evening appointment. When I got in the car, I was angry, crying, and furious. I had never contemplated divorce, but I wished Marshall would have said the word that day because I would have grabbed it and run as fast as possible.

As I pull out of the driveway, I slipped a Twyla Paris cassette into the player (yes, this story is that old). As I heard the words of the song, God began to soften my heart. The words spoke of God not giving up on someone who kept making the same mistakes and closed with the statement, "neither will I". It was a clear message from the Lord; I was to fight for my marriage and our relationship.

Malachi 2:16 teaches, "God hates divorce." But sometimes, divorce is the only answer. God does, however, love both people involved in the conflict and wants the best for them separately and together. As believers, we must do everything we possibly can to not only reconcile but create a harmonious living environment. We must do everything we can to love and honor our commitment to one another and to God.

Marta

DAY 8
GOD'S LOVINGKINDNESS

"How precious is Thy lovingkindness, O God!"
Psalm 36:7

The Bible describes King David as "a man after God's own heart" (1 Sam 13:14; Acts 13:22).

It does not describe David as perfect or as one who never sinned. He did know God's laws and ways and did strive to follow what he knew to be right. David wrote about people who seemed to be focused only on themselves and "do not despise evil" Psalm 36:4.

David changed and began to praise God for being faithful in loving those who love Him and judging those who follow their own ways. Psalm 36:6-7 recounts, "Thy righteousness is like the mountains of God; Thy judgments are like a great deep. O Lord, Thou preservest man and beast. How precious is Thy lovingkindness, O God! And the children of men take refuge in the shadow of Thy wings."

Can you imagine resting in the shadow of God's wings? I want that feeling. I want to feel the overwhelming peace and 100% protection of Our Father. I want to be so filled with the lovingkindness of God that

not one other thing enters my thoughts. I love the outdoors and feel the love of our Savior in a beautiful sunset or sunrise. I feel at such peace when I am on a beach on a sunny day with my toes in the sand, the sun on my face, the breeze cooling me, and the sound of waves lapping the shore. Have you been snow skiing? That is another place where I feel so small yet free and covered by the wings of God. All these things are gifts from the One who loves me and loves you!

Each of us has a place where we are filled with His lovingkindness, where is yours?

Maureen

REFLECTION

1. Where is the place you feel most in harmony with Our Lord?

2. Is there a time when you especially felt you were in the safety of His wings?

3. Note one thing you can do today to show God's love to a stranger, then do it!

DAY 9
WINTER

"But as for me, I shall sing of Thy strength; Yes, I shall joyfully sing of Thy lovingkindness in the morning, for thou hast been my stronghold, And a refuge in the day of my distress."
Psalm 59:16

It had been one of the coldest winters in Texas history, and I believe it was a season when we were to sit up and take notice!

Four million Texans lost electric power, water, and gas for days. There were no electronics. A glance outside showed a barren landscape, a frozen land. It would have been easy to feel despair, but I saw hope!

We are blessed to have many trees in our yard, some at least a hundred years old. One fascinates me. It is a large 60-year-old tree that grows crooked! It leans so far I think it may fall, but still, it stands. Surrounding trees grow straight and tall. During the cold winter, these trees had only a touch of snow on their branches and none on their trunks. The crooked tree, however, had a thick layer of snow on its branches, and even the trunk was covered.

This tree reminds me of King David. It is vital and will live many years, but it has become bent over time. Because of how this tree has grown, it carried an

enormous burden of snow, unlike the trees that have grown straight. Because of our life decisions, we become "crooked" and often carry heavy loads. We simply need to stand straight in the Father's

love. Psalm 59:16 praises, "But as for me, I shall sing of Thy strength; Yes, I shall joyfully sing of Thy lovingkindness in the morning, for thou hast been my stronghold and a refuge in the day of my distress."

The sun always comes out and melts the snow from the tree. It then springs back to life, grows green leaves, becomes a home for birds and squirrels, and provides shade for us. Because of the lovingkindness of our Father, who gave us His only Son, we are being released from the burdens of our hearts. Out of our winter is the spring of Jesus, bringing us new life and allowing us to flourish.

Don't stay in your winter covered with heavy burdens. Instead, come into your spring and walk in freedom with the One who loves you!

REFLECTION

1. What burdens are keeping you "bent over"?

2. Close your eyes and imagine the warm sun shining to melt your burdens and the loving arms of Jesus wrapped around you.

3. What steps will you take to help you grow straight in your walk with Jesus?

DAY 10
DESERT PRAISES

"Because Thy lovingkindness is better than life, my lips will praise Thee."
Psalm 63:3

Scholars believe David was in the desert when he wrote this Psalm to the Lord.

They imagine David wrote this while living in the desert, being chased by Saul, or when he was in brief exile from the throne during the rebellion of his son, Absalom. Regardless, David was in a desert, both literally and figuratively.

In verses 1-2, David tells God his soul thirsts for Him, and his flesh longs for Him, "Even in a dry and thirsty land where there is no water." In verse 3, "Because Your lovingkindness is better than life, my lips will glorify you," David believed God's great love was a gift and that it was "better than life." David valued God's love and would sacrifice for it. People give love to one another. David wanted to express God's great love. No matter what occurred in David's life, he praised God with his lips.

What about you? Have you been in a dry, thirsty land in summer? I lived in Arizona six years. This California girl never expected to live in a desert,

but God had other plans. The first time I walked outside into 120 degrees, it felt like I had walked into an oven. Historical heat records were broken during my first summer in the desert.

God's great love took me to that "dry" period in my life and taught me to cling to Him. As David, I had to believe in my soul to see and feel God's lovingkindness. I was invited to join a weekly Bible study. My knowledge of the Word and my love of God grew exponentially. I learned to value this amazing love of God, though I had to sacrifice (in my case, time) to learn that love. I wanted everyone to feel this complete love. Listening exclusively to Christian music, I soon learned beautiful songs of praise.

David was in the desert, but he never hesitated to praise God. It is a lifelong goal to learn to proclaim that the love of God is greater than one's own life.

REFLECTION

1. Describe a time when you were in a "dry" place. Where were you, and what were you doing?

2. What refreshed you during this time (people, scenery, etc.)?

3. What have you done since then to share God's love with others?

DAY 11
FOLLY

"Show us Thy lovingkindness, O Lord, and grant us Thy Salvation. I will hear what the Lord will say; For He will speak peace to His people, to His godly ones; but let them not turn back to folly."
Psalm 85:7-8

The psalmist described the Lord's favor in the past.

Some believe this was written at the time when the Jews returned from their captivity in Babylon. Verses 1-6 remind the Lord of the mercies He had shown his people: He restored the fortunes of Jacob (1), forgave everyone's sins (2), and turned away from His fierce anger (3). In verse 7, he asks God to "Show us Thy lovingkindness, O Lord, and grant us Thy Salvation." Verse 8 says, "I will hear what the Lord will say; For He will speak peace to His people, to His godly ones; But let them not turn back to folly."

The word "folly" is defined in the dictionary as a "lack of good sense" or "foolishness." It is an old-fashioned word that has significant meaning today as I reflect on what is happening worldwide. This Psalm is our warning. It

describes all the good that will come to the man who follows the ways of the Lord. The land will yield produce, and the Lord will give what is good.

However, what happens when we turn to folly? Old Testament history warns how God often reacts to people who turn from Him. Sodom and Gomorrah were destroyed, the world flooded, the Jews were taken captive, etc. What will happen today to those living with foolishness or "folly"?

Is it folly to live each day trying to please others instead of pleasing God? Is it folly to follow the radical thinking of many of the accepted patterns of the world instead of those of The Lord?

Look at your life today. Search your heart. Are you making decisions that lack good sense? Turn your heart back to the One who loves you the most! Turn your heart back to Jesus.

REFLECTION

1. List three times the Lord has shown you lovingkindness in your life.

2. Is there something in your heart that could be considered folly in the eyes of the Lord?

3. What steps will you take to change your heart?

UNLOVABLE
MY STORY

As I prepared to write this story, I clearly understood God wanted me to write about loving people who are often difficult to love. You know who they are in your life, the ones who drive you crazy and wish would vanish.

I believe God put these people in our lives for our good. In Luke 6:27, we are told, "But I say to you who hear, love your enemies, do good to those who hate you." Verse 31 is very explicit, "And just as you want people to treat you, treat them in the same way." The Bible is not telling us to treat well only those people we love, but everyone! That, my friends, is difficult.

I have been friends with the Smith family for thirty years. They have lost a son to alcoholism and have accepted and continued to love a son who has professed homosexuality. The mother has had a severe injury  and consequent knee surgery and rehabilitation. It has now become time to make decisions about long-term care for the patriarch of the family, whose health is physically and mentally declining.

The burden of this decision lies on the eldest daughter, Veronica. Here's the clincher…. the aging father has never been very nice to his daughter. He has blamed her for the bad choices her siblings have made and never respected that she has taken good care of the family finances and kept a roof over their heads. He has become a very insensitive person. He berates her and anyone trying to help him. He argues with the caregivers. He fights kindness and love every step of the way.

Many people face this dilemma, and many walk away from the complex parts of life. However, Veronica works daily with caregivers and therapists to help her

father regain strength and continue to live independently. She checks on him several times daily and ensures he is clean and eats healthy food. She tells him she loves him and only wants the best for him. I highly respect this friend and believe she is representing the love of Jesus to her father. John 13:35 "By this all men will know that you are my disciples, if you have love for one another."

Matthew 5:43-45 teaches, "You have heard that it was said, 'You shall love your neighbor[, and hate your enemy.' 'But I say to you, love your enemies, and pray for those who persecute you, in order that you may be sons of your Father who is in heaven." As believers of Jesus Christ, we are called to love the unlovable. This is not a suggestion but an attribute that identifies us as believers.

Ra`ah

הָעֳר

To pasture

"From very ancient antiquity, rulers were described as demonstrating their legitimacy to rule by their ability to "pasture" their people. Hammurabi and many other rulers of ancient western Asia are called "shepherd" or described as "pasturing" their subjects. In the OT, however, it is the Lord who feeds his people and is praised for his mercy in providing for them (Gen 48:15; Ps 23:1; 28:9; Isa 40:11; Hos 4:16 et al). This attribute of God is one of the marks of the offices of prophets, priest, and king. David's claim to the throne is based upon God's command that he feed the people (II Sam 5:2). Failure of the officers of Israel to feed the people either physical or spiritual nourishment was deemed a severe transgression (Ezk 34:2ff.) In this chapter the prophet plays repeatedly on the two forms of the root, rāʿâ, the verb meaning "to pasture" and the noun meaning the "pastor" or shepherd. The true repetition of the ideas is lost in all the versions by supplying synonyms where the Hebrew uses the same term throughout. The OT theological vision of the good shepherd who feeds his flock with God's truth (Jer 3:15 etc.) becomes prominent in the NT (Jn 10:11)."[1]

---

1   William White, "2185 הָעַר," ed. R. Laird Harris, Gleason L. Archer Jr., and Bruce K. Waltke, *Theological Wordbook of the Old Testament* (Chicago: Moody Press, 1999), 853.

DAY 12
A SHEPHERD'S LOVE

"And Samuel said to Jesse, "Are these all the children?" And he said, "There remains yet the youngest, and behold, he is tending the sheep." Then Samuel said to Jesse, "Send and bring him; for we will not sit down until he comes here.""
1 Samuel 16:11

How interesting that God connects love with being a shepherd.

God tells Samuel, 1 Samuel 16, He will reveal the future King of Israel. The Lord leads Samuel to Jesse's home in Bethlehem. Of Jessie's oldest, he thinks, "Surely the Lord's anointed is before Him" (Verse 6). God exclaims, "But the Lord said to Samuel, "Do not look at his appearance or at the height of his stature, because I have rejected him; for God sees not as man sees, for man looks at the outward appearance, but the Lord looks at the heart." (1 Samuel 16:7). Samuel learned how God considers people for leadership, not how man chooses leaders.

Jesse's sons passed before Samuel one by one, and the Lord rejected each one. Finally, Samuel asked, "Are these all the children?" (Verse 11). Even David's father, Jessie, never conceived his youngest son could be the future king; after all, David was merely a shepherd boy.

Yet, God had been training David from a young age. What did he learn? He learned how to care for the weak and helpless, those who couldn't take care of themselves. He realized he had to lay down his life for his sheep, sometimes fighting bears. His job was to protect the sheep at all costs, and the sheep would trust and rely on their shepherd.

God's training ground for leadership usually looks different from the world's training. David's started with him learning to love and care for the weakest and defenseless. God wants to raise an army of leaders for a lost and helpless generation that needs to know Him. We must learn to love like a shepherd, THE shepherd, to impact the next generation.

REFLECTION

1. Who has been shepherding you and leading you closer to God's love? Describe how this has happened.

2. God wants every person to be a leader in His army. How is He working on your leadership skills?

3. What has God trained you to do? Are you doing it?

Yādîd

דִּידְיָ

One greatly loved

"The basic meaning of the noun is "one greatly loved" by God or by man. The noun is derived from the verb "love" (ydd) (BDB; KB).

This noun is primarily employed to describe the nation of Israel (or Judah) and individuals as those who are greatly loved by the Lord. Such love by God brings protection (cf. Benjamin; Deut 33:12) and prosperity (Ps 127:2) upon the beloved people. This love demonstrates the reason for God's continual faithfulness to his people Israel, even when they were disobedient and unfaithful (Jer 11:15). It is upon the basis of this love of God for Israel that she petitions for the Lord to hear and deliver her from judgment (Ps 60:5 [H 7]; 108:6 [H 7]). Isaiah describes the Lord, the vinedresser of unfaithful Israel, as his beloved (Isa 5:1), showing his great love for the Lord. The psalmist rejoices in the temple dwellings as "lovely" (or "beloved"), i.e. the place where he delights to worship the Lord."[1]

---

[1] Ralph H. Alexander, "846 ידד," ed. R. Laird Harris, Gleason L. Archer Jr., and Bruce K. Waltke, *Theological Wordbook of the Old Testament* (Chicago: Moody Press, 1999), 364.

DAY 13
LOVELY DWELLING PLACES

"How lovely are Thy dwelling places, O Lord of hosts! My soul longed and even yearned for the courts of the Lord; My heart and my flesh sing for joy to the living God"
(Psalm 84:1-2)

*H*ave you ever felt as if you didn't belong?

For a follower of Jesus, this is not an absurd question. Everyone has a sense of needing to belong and feel at home. Home is safe. Home is comfort. It's a natural instinct to go to great lengths to make our family and friends feel comfortable in our home.

Psalm 84 echoes this sentiment, "How lovely are Thy dwelling places, O Lord of hosts! My soul longed and even yearned for the courts of the Lord; My heart and my flesh sing for joy to the living God" (Psalm 84:1-2). God goes to great lengths for us to feel at home. For a child of the living God, His courts are part of our home, this is where we should feel safe and comfortable. This is where we should long to be. His courts are part of our eternal reward where we will spend eternity with Him.

When we feel as if we don't belong, it's because we're not home yet! God creates a home in our hearts. God's heart is relationship. He wants intimacy with His people.

Remember when you dated someone you loved? You longed to talk with them and listened intently to their every word. This is who God should be to us. He is the one we can run to when we are lonely, insecure, or feeling out of place. He will lovingly listen and take us into His courts to comfort and console us. "For a day in Thy courts is better than a thousand outside. I would rather stand at the threshold of the house of my God, than dwell in the tents of wickedness" (Psalm 84:10).

Marta

REFLECTION

1. Are you longing for Him?

2. Where do you feel most comfortable? Where do you feel like you belong?

3. How do you welcome someone new into your circle of love?

rāḥam

Love for Jehovah

"Rāḥam is used only once in the Qal when the Psalmist confesses his love for Jehovah (18:1).

There are several ideas attached to God's deep, tender love: first, the unconditional election of God (Ex 33:19); next, his mercy and forgiveness toward his people in the face of deserved judgment and upon the condition of their repentance (Deut 13:17); also, God's continuing mercy and grace in preserving his unrepentant people from judgment (II Kgs 13:23). Thus this attribute becomes the basis in part of an eschatological hope (cf. Isa 14:1; 49:13; 54:7; Jer 12:15; 33:26; Ezk 34:25; Mic 7:19; Zech 1:16). It is noteworthy that Deuteronomy (30:3) prophesies the exile because of Israel's sin, stipulating that repentance will meet with God's tender compassion. So we read of the withdrawal of God's mercy resulting in harsh judgment at the hands of Babylon (Isa 9:17 [H 16]; 27:11; Hos 2:4). During the exile Israel's leaders encouraged the people with God's electing love and tender-mercy (Lam 3:32), and led them in humbling themselves in repentance, calling upon God to reinstate his fatherlike compassion (Zech 1:12). The restitution of the father-son relationship and the return from the exile witnesses this accompanying loving care (Hos 2:23). Scripture makes it certain that the exile was brought by God and terminated by God (Ezk 39:25) according to his sovereign providence (Isa 30:18; cf. E. J. Young, The Book of Isaiah, II, p. 353f.). Finally, the prophets' message regarding the return from the exile opens onto a permanent state where the father-son relationship will never be broken (Hos 2:23; Isa 54:8, 10)."[1]

---

[1] Leonard J. Coppes, "2146 רחם," ed. R. Laird Harris, Gleason L. Archer Jr., and Bruce K. Waltke, *Theological Wordbook of the Old Testament* (Chicago: Moody Press, 1999), 841–842.

DAY 14

GRACIOUS COMPASSIONATE LOVE

"The Lord longs to be gracious to you, and therefore He waits on high to have compassion on you. For the Lord is a God of justice; How blessed are all those who long for Him."
Isaiah 30:18

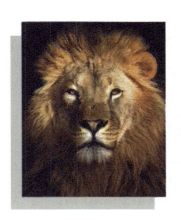

Isaiah 30:1 declares, "Woe to the rebellious children," declares the Lord, "Who execute a plan, but not Mine, and make an alliance, but not of My Spirit, in order to add sin to sin."

Isaiah was a prophet with a challenging message. He was to tell the Southern Kingdom, Judah, to return to the Lord or He would send them into the hands of their enemies.

300 years earlier, Israel had chosen an earthly king, "that we also may be like all the nations" (1 Samuel 8:20). Instead of trusting and serving the King of kings, the children of Israel were far from the Lord and His commandments. Isaiah was told by the Lord, "do not omit a word" (Jeremiah 26:2) of the Lord's message for Judah. Today, we know Israel, the Northern Kingdom, had been taken captive by Assyria; and Judah, the Southern Kingdom, was one hundred years from being captured by King Nebuchadnezzar of Babylon.

Was there something Judah could have done to prevent capture and slavery to a pagan king? Isaiah 30:15 reveals, "'In repentance and rest you shall  be saved, in quietness and trust is your strength.' But you were not willing." This passage clearly warned of the key to Judah's salvation, repentance. But regrettably, it also tells us they were not willing. This principle is as true today as it was for Judah, regardless of whether we are talking about an individual relationship with the Lord, or a nation or people group. Salvation lies in repentance. Freedom lies in repentance.

Mercifully we have a God who is always available. He is a God who will show up when we stop being stiff-necked and rebellious. Isaiah 30:18 reassures us, "Therefore the Lord longs to be gracious to you, and therefore He waits on high to have compassion on you. For the Lord is a God of justice; How blessed are all those who long for Him." God loves us, so He heaps compassion and mercy on we who repent and turn to Him. He is a God who will never forsake those who trust in Him.

REFLECTION

1. In what area(s) of your life have you have been rebellious and unwilling to follow the Lord?

2. What do you think of the fact that the Lord longs to have compassion on you (and others)?

3. Are you willing to follow the Lord? What steps will you take?

agápé

ἀγαπάω

To have love for someone or something

To have love for someone or something, based on sincere appreciation and high regard— 'to love, to regard with affection, loving concern, love.' ἀγαπάωa: ἐντολὴν καινὴν δίδωμι ὑμῖν, ἵνα ἀγαπᾶτε ἀλλήλους 'I give you a new commandment, that you love one another' Jn 13:34; γὰρ τὸν ἕνα μισήσει καὶ τὸν ἕτερον ἀγαπήσει 'for he will hate the one and love the other' Lk 16:13; ὁ πατὴρ ἀγαπᾷ τὸν υἱόν 'the Father loves the Son' Jn 3:35; ὅτι αὐτὸς πρῶτος ἠγάπησεν ἡμᾶς 'for he loved us first' 1 Jn 4:19.

ἀγάπηa: ἡ ἀγάπη οὐδέποτε πίπτει 'love does not fail' 1 Cor 13:8; ἡ ἀγάπη τῷ πλησίον κακὸν οὐκ ἐργάζεται 'a person who loves doesn't do evil to his neighbor' Ro 13:10.

Though some persons have tried to assign certain significant differences of meaning between ἀγαπάωa, ἀγάπηa and φιλέωa, φιλία (25.33), it does not seem possible to insist upon a contrast of meaning in any and all contexts. For

example, the usage in Jn 21:15–17 seems to reflect simply a rhetorical alternation designed to avoid undue repetition. There is, however, one significant clue to possible meaningful differences in at least some contexts, namely, the fact that people are never commanded to love one another with φιλέω or φιλία, but only with ἀγαπάω and ἀγάπη. Though the meanings of these terms overlap considerably in many contexts, there are probably some significant differences in certain contexts; that is to say, φιλέω and φιλία are likely to focus upon love or affection based upon interpersonal association, while ἀγαπάω and ἀγάπη focus upon love and affection based on deep appreciation and high regard. On the basis of this type of distinction, one can understand some of the reasons for the use of ἀγαπάω and ἀγάπη in commands to Christians to love one another. It would,  however, be quite wrong to assume that φιλέω and φιλία refer only to human love, while ἀγαπάω and ἀγάπη refer to divine love. Both sets of terms are used for the total range of loving relations between people, between people and God, and between God and Jesus Christ.[1]

---

[1] Johannes P. Louw and Eugene Albert Nida, <u>Greek-English Lexicon of the New Testament: Based on Semantic Domains</u> (New York: United Bible Societies, 1996), 292–293.

MY TP FRIEND

OUR STORY
PART ONE

You may not think of buying toilet paper for someone is an expression of love, but in my case, it's very true. There are several reasons why the lack of toilet paper was one of my few fears.

My husband and I lived in Romania for many years. When we first arrived, the toilet paper was terrible! It was like crepe paper and industrial brown filled with tiny wood splinters.

As a result, Americans who came to visit had to bring American toilet paper.

Who would think running low on toilet paper could be so stressful? Years later, stores in larger cities stocked better quality toilet paper. We only went to the big city once a month, and ensuring we had enough toilet paper to last for the month was tricky.

Upon our return to America, we experienced several lean financial years. The old stress of running out of toilet paper reared its ugly head. This is when I met Maureen. How she found out about my shortage of toilet paper fear, I don't know, but Maureen began to bring me large quantities of toilet paper: the huge 48 rolls in one bag you buy from the big box stores.

She would show up just in time with 48 rolls of love. Maureen's care and attention of me in this area ministered to me in ways I can't describe. She loved me where I was and helped me with my irrational fear of running out of toilet paper. She has been a true friend to me from the first day we met, and her tangible expressions of love are always noticed and appreciated.

I hope God sends you a toilet paper friend who will minister to you in such loving and unique ways. I hope you pray to become a toilet paper friend to someone in need.

Marta

OUR STORY PART TWO

M arta and her husband stayed with us briefly while waiting for their new home.

During this time, her husband wondered what kind of toilet paper I bought. This prompted a funny conversation about the importance of soft toilet paper, more importantly, the availability of any toilet paper. Marta shared her Romanian experience with me, and I made a silent promise to ensure my friend always had the necessary type and number of toilet paper rolls!

This has continued over our eleven-year friendship, and we laugh each time I show up with 48 rolls of love! Yes, it is a practical gift, but to Marta, it is an expression of love, and to me, it is a joy to be able to show her love in this way.

Jesus fed the hungry, healed the sick, and loved all people. He is our ultimate example of showing love in extraordinary and practical ways.

DAY 15
JESUS' LOVE

"I say to you, love your enemies, and pray for those who persecute you."
Matthew 5:44

Jesus' first recorded teaching is the Sermon on the Mount.

By then, He had quite a following. Large crowds followed because of the healings He performed (Matthew 4:23-24). His instructions were controversial, such as,  "Blessed are you when men cast insults at you, and persecute you (Matthew 5:11)." He also upset the religious leaders by preaching reconciliation with one's brother (vs. 24) and making friends with opponents (vs.25).

I can imagine people in the crowds looking at one another, even whispering. Jesus' teaching was so radical and contentious that eventually, John 6:66 tells us, *"As a result of this many of His disciples withdrew, and were not walking with Him anymore."* Then as now, disciples make choices as to whom to serve and follow.

Today, the world chooses tolerance over repentance. A biblical worldview calls a believer to live a righteous and holy life; a life set apart or sanctified. We find ourselves in conflict with the world when we choose God. The Bible states clearly, the more we become like Jesus, the more the world struggles with our decision. We may find our friends and even family withdrawing from us, just as they did with Jesus.

How do we handle this? Jesus taught, *"You have heard that it was said, 'You shall love your neighbor and hate your enemy.' But I say to you, love your enemies and pray for those who persecute you."* He tells us the "why" in

Matthew 5:43-45a, *"So that you may be sons of your Father who is in heaven."* As sons and daughters of the God Most High, we must choose a different path, a different road. In a world that divides, we must love. Love doesn't divide, it only multiplies. Love and prayer can change an enemy into a convert of Jesus Christ, a Saul into a Paul, through the power of the Holy Spirit.

REFLECTION

1. What does "Love like Jesus" mean according to this Scripture?

2. For whom has God called you to pray? How has this affected your prayer life?

3. Send an e-mail to info@wogt.org to let us know how we can pray for you.

DAY 16
PUREST LOVE

"For God so loved the world, that He gave His only begotten Son, that whoever believes in Him shall not perish, but have eternal life."
John 3:16

When it comes to God's love, ágape love, we humans think it's complicated.

Why? Because our feelings get in the way. What do I mean? God's ágape love is desiring God's best for someone, not what we, as humans, think is best.

Judging by emotions can cause confusion, particularly using a modern-day standard of love and tolerance as a plumbline. For example, an alcoholic may say he needs another drink to make it through the day. Someone having an ágape love for the alcoholic would know that is not true and suggest help to stop drinking. The alcoholic could respond, "You don't love me!" yet you are expressing the purest form of love. You are doing what is best for the person instead of doing what he wants.

God's love focuses on the end result, which is, first and foremost, eternity. God loves us enough to make provision for our eternity. God knew many would reject His Son as deliverance from their sins. Yet God still sent His Son, His only Son, to die for the sins of the world, especially for those who reject God's precious gift of salvation.

In Luke 19, when Jesus rode into Jerusalem on Palm Sunday 2,000 years ago, the people wanted a king to save them from their tyrannical king. They wanted an earthly king to protect them. But

God didn't give them what they wanted; He gave them what they needed. They didn't need a king; they needed a Savior, someone who sacrificed for their sins to provide them eternal life. God had an eternal kingdom in their future, but first, His Son, Jesus, needed to pay the price for the world's sins. Therefore, He gave them what they needed, not what they wanted. One day in the future, God's children will see the kingdom that Israel desired so many years ago. Father, teach us to love as You love.

Marta

REFLECTION

1. How often has God given you ágape?

2. Were you even aware of God's grace in your life?

3. When you are involved in the lives of others, do you give them what they need, or what they want? How much do you love them?

DAY 17
FOLLOW THE COMMANDMENTS

"He who has My commandments and keeps them, he it is who loves Me; and he who loves Me shall be loved by My Father, and I will love him and will disclose Myself to him."
John 14:21

Many passages in the book of John speak of love.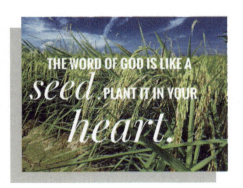

Wanting His disciples to be confident in His love for them, Jesus spoke to His apostles in John 14. Jesus assured them in verses 18-20, He will not leave theme as orphans, that they would live because He lived, and they would know Jesus lives in the Father and the Father in Him.

Jesus addressed everyone when He said, "He who has My commandments and keeps them, he it is who loves Me; and he who loves Me shall be loved by My Father, and I will love him and will disclose Myself to him," John 14:21.

Can you believe it? All that is required of us is to keep the commandments, and God will know we love Him. He will then "disclose" Himself to us. One meaning of "disclose" is "impart." This means God loves us so much that He will live in us, and we will have Jesus imparted into our souls.

This seems such an enormous concept to grasp, but it is quite simple. As the scripture says, follow the commandments, the rest is already a promise by God.

The 10 Commandments of God (Exodus 20:3-18 & Deuteronomy 5:7-21)

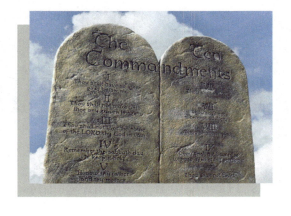

1. I am the Lord your God; you shall have no other gods before me.

2. You shall not make for yourself idols, nor worship idols.

3. You shall not take the name of the Lord your God in vain.

4. Remember the sabbath day to keep it holy.

5. Honor your father and your mother.

6. You shall not murder.

7. You shall not commit adultery.

8. You shall not steal.

9. You shall not bear false witness against your neighbor.

10. You shall not covet.

REFLECTION

1. Have you broken any of these commandments (I know I have)? List the ones that are the most difficult for you.

2. Write a prayer asking for help to overcome temptation.

3. Spend a few minutes in silence and solitude, relishing in the love of Our Savior.

DAY 18
GREATER LOVE

"Greater love has no one than this, that one lay down his life for his friends."
John 15:13

The account of Jesus' last Passover with His disciples, just before the crucifixion, begins in John 13.

After Judas slipped away to betray the Messiah, Jesus held a final exchange with the remaining eleven before being taken to the cross. We find this conversation in God's Word in John 13:31 through John 17:26.

As with any final conversation with a loved one, we treasure Jesus' words. A keyword throughout the exchange is "love." Jesus said, "A new commandment I give to you, that you love one another, even as I have loved you, that you also love one another. By this all men will know that you are My disciples, if you have love for one another." John 13:34-35.

An essential attribute of Jesus' disciples is love for one another. A disciple is a follower embodying and applying the teachings of another. So, if we profess to be a disciple of Jesus, we love as He loved.

Jesus taught the apostles about the greatest love in John 15:13,"Greater love has no one than this, that a person will lay down his life for his friends." Regrettably, His disciples still did not understand He would soon lay down His life, not only for His friends but for those who would even reject and say they hate Him.

Jesus demonstrated the greatest love for humanity when He laid down His life for the world's sins 2,000 years ago. This kind of love is challenging. Jesus has called you to demonstrate love like His. In a world that seems to be all about the "me, me, me," Jesus commanded us to be in radical opposition to that attitude and to lay down our lives.

REFLECTION

1. How did you respond when Jesus commanded you to be "all in?"

2. How can you demonstrate Jesus' love in your daily life?

3. When has someone exhibited Jesus' love to you?

DAY 19

GOD DEMONSTRATED HIS LOVE

"But God demonstrates His own love toward us, in that while we were yet sinners, Christ died for us."
Romans 5:8

The book of Romans is filled with references to the love of our God for us.

For example, chapter 5:8 says, "But God demonstrates His own love toward us, in that while we were yet sinners, Christ died for us." Yes, my friends, He died for you, and He died for me, those we love, and those we do not even like.

He did this even though we are all sinners!

It is not easy to do nice things for people who mistreat us. But that doesn't matter with God. He knows all the good, the bad, and the ugly of each of us. He knows we do not always follow His commandments. He knows we often choose man's rules over His rules. While Jesus was being tortured, and as He hung on the cross, He prayed for those who were crucifying Him. Jesus proclaimed, "Father, forgive them; for they do not know what they are doing," Luke 23:34.

That is love. That is also the kind of love demonstrated by our men and women in the military and law enforcement. They are called on daily to lay down their lives for strangers. My grandson, Dustin, is in the army and is prepared to follow orders and put himself in harm's way at a moment's notice.

That is the kind of love we are to demonstrate to one another daily. It is difficult, but do you think it was effortless for Jesus to endure suffering and death? He is God, but on earth, Jesus was fully man. He left his heavenly home where he lived in communion with His Father and angels to live on earth as an ordinary man. Think about that the next time God calls you to do something out of your comfort zone for His Kingdom.

Remember, God loves you no matter what. You can show your love for Him by listening to Him and obeying His commands.

REFLECTION

1. Have you left your comfort zone to follow God's prompting? How? When?

2. Was your effort graciously received?

3. Write a prayer for one who has hurt you, but whom God is asking you to hand over to Him.

ANGELS AMONG US

MY STORY

In the mid-nineteen-nineties, I wasn't a seasoned traveler. I was headed to Chicago's Cook County Jail with hundreds of other ministers to share the good news of Jesus Christ with those held captive. But I had a plan, or so I thought. Upon  arrival, the ministry I was serving with had transportation waiting to take me to the hotel.

The plane was four hours late, and no one was there to meet me. When I phoned the ministry, everyone was already gone for the day. I didn't know the name or location of the hotel; as I said, I wasn't a seasoned traveler. And to make matters worse, I had very little cash with me. I was in a world of hurt. So, what was I going to do?

I said a frantic 911 prayer, the one where you cry out to the Lord in desperation. At that moment, I saw a very tall elderly woman in tattered clothes, looking quite lost. I thought to help her, what else did I have to do? I quickly realized she didn't speak English. I looked at her ticket and led her to her gate.

After fifteen minutes, we arrived at her gate, there I saw a man wearing a hat with the ministry name of the organization I was serving with for the weekend. I turned to the man, asked him to hold up for a moment, and then turned around to say my goodbyes to the woman. She had vanished! It had only been a few seconds.

Hebrews 1:14 teaches, "Are they (angels), not all ministering spirits, sent out to render service for the sake of those who will inherit salvation?" God sent me His angel to help me in my time of need. No one will convince me otherwise. God's love for us is so vast and unmeasurable that we may never be able to comprehend this side of heaven and how much He cares for us and attends to our every need.

DAY 20
SUFFERING LOVE

"We know that God causes all things to work together for good to those who love God, to those who are called according to His purpose."
Romans 8:28

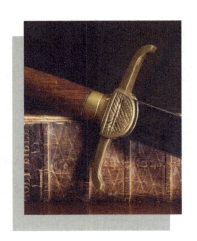

Many claim Romans 8:28 as their "life verse." Who wouldn't want God to work all things out for our good?

But studying this passage in the context of Romans, many do not have a proper understanding of Paul's teaching.

Chapter eight of Romans addresses not walking according to the flesh, being dead to sin, and walking alive by the Spirit. Paul exhorts that we are heirs with Christ if we suffer with Him to glorify us (Romans 8:17) and, Romans 8:18, "For I consider that the sufferings of this present time are not worthy to be compared with the glory that is to be revealed to us."

This context unmistakably explains suffering as part of the Christian life. Paul boldly states in verse 35, "Who shall separate us from the love of Christ?" He then lists possible scenarios in which we may be found tribulation, distress, persecution, famine, nakedness, peril or sword. These situations are not what the American church imagines when we speak of living for Christ. We believe this happens in other countries or possibly at another time. Paul wants to make it clear to us that despite our circumstances, God loves us!

Paul further emphasizes his stand on suffering as he quotes Psalm 44:22, "For thy sake we are killed all day long; we are considered as sheep to be slaughtered." Are we willing to lay down our lives just as Christ did for us?

His final thought begins, "In all things we overwhelmingly conquer through Him who loved us" (Romans 8:37). In studying Romans, the context suggests Romans 8:28 is teaching us that God will work His purpose in and through our suffering for the benefit of the kingdom of God. Why? Because we love Him. But how can that be? Because He first loved us (1 John 4:19).

REFLECTION

1. When did you first sense God's love?

2. Is there a time when God allowed something difficult in your life to be used for good?

3. Have you ever suffered because you loved Jesus? Explain.

DAY 21
LOVE NEVER FAILS

"Love never fails; but if there are gifts of prophecy, they will be done away; if there are tongues, they will cease; if there is knowledge, it will be done away."
1 Cor. 13:8

Paul addressed the Corinthian church to explain the never-ending love of God.

Having been taught God's love since birth, this concept is easy for me to appreciate. As this scripture clearly promises, all else will fail, but love endures.

"Love never fails; but if there are gifts of prophecy, they will be done away; if there are tongues, they will cease; if there is knowledge, it will be done away" 1 *Corinthians 13:8*. In this passage, the words *"never"* and *"will"* resonated with my spirit. Love never fails, but everything else will fail. That is a promise, and God always keeps His promises! So, let's think about things that have failed.

A turning point in my life came when my marriage to the father of my children ended in divorce. I believed that the relationship would last forever, but it did not. The trust failed, the security failed, and my pride failed. I was ashamed, hurt, financially broken, and emotionally devastated. I had two daughters to raise, so

I picked myself up and put one foot in front of the other and carried on! My family was immensely supportive, and I began to trust the One who would never stop loving me.

All who know me know my most peaceful place on earth is at the beach, any beach, soaking in the glory of God. I was recently standing in the waves of the Pacific Ocean.

It was a sunny day with bright blue skies. The small waves gently rolled onto shore. I thanked God for all the beauty surrounding me, relishing in the continual, never-ending waves softly washing onto the beach.

I realized the water will never stop coming to shore, and waves will never stop breaking on the beach. It is precisely the same with God's love, He will NEVER stop loving you, ever.

REFLECTION

1. Name a time something or someone failed or disappointed you.

2. How did you respond?

3. Trusting God's love, how would you have handled it differently?

DAY 22
FAITH IN LOVE

"For in Christ Jesus neither circumcision nor uncircumcision means anything, but faith working through love."
Galatians 5:6

The apostle Paul's first letter was written to the church at Galatia because false prophets were preaching their own version of the gospel of Jesus Christ.

Paul was very attached to the people in this town, which is modern-day Turkey. He was shocked they were not following the actual teachings of Jesus.

This book covers six chapters with three main themes: protecting the gospel, clarifying the gospel, and walking out the gospel.

Paul asked in Galatians 1:10, "For am I now seeking the favor of men, or of God? Or am I striving to please men?" Then as now, this cautions that we are to please only God. These words jump off the page at me, screaming this is precisely what is happening today. How many of us are striving to please man instead of God?

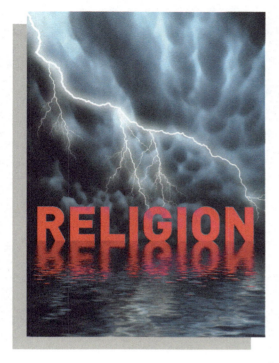

Chapters 3 and 4 found Paul reminding the church that they will be saved by faith alone in Jesus Christ, not by works. This was a challenge to the Jewish people who had lived under the law for generations. Galatians 3:13 declares, "Christ redeemed us from the curse of the Law, having become a curse for us." Jesus Christ became the new covenant for all humanity.

In Galatians 5:6 Paul explained the old rituals and practices no longer mattered, "For in Christ Jesus neither circumcision nor uncircumcision means anything, but faith working through love." People who believe God loves them, in and through Jesus, will respond by loving God and then loving others.

REFLECTION

1. Whom are you trying to please or impress instead of God (e.g., with expensive clothes, car, trips, etc.)?

2. On your deathbed, what will you regret?

3. How is God showing His love for you today?

DAY 23
LOVE DURING TRIALS

"And may the Lord cause you to increase and abound in love for one another, and for all men, just as we also do for you."
1 Thessalonians 3:12

The apostle Paul, Timothy, and Silas believed they were to go to Phillipi.

Upon arrival, they were beaten and imprisoned. The trio then traveled to Thessalonica, where they preached, and many came to believe. Persecution was directed not only at them but anyone who accepted Christ as Lord and Savior. Trouble followed wherever they went, and Paul was concerned people would be discouraged. The three disciples visited other cities as well to spread the Word and escape persecution.

Paul wrote his first letter to the church of Thessalonica in 51 A.D. I sincerely enjoy how Paul began his letters, sending well wishes to his fellow believers and thanking God for them. Paul demonstrated his love and care toward those who would hear his words. He reminded them in chapter 1 he knew they had been filled with the Holy Spirit, and they were "examples to all the believers in Macedonia and Achaia," 1 Thessalonians 1:7.

Paul reminded the Thessalonians in chapter 3 he was no longer with them because he could not endure the suffering. He wrote, "the tempter might have tempted you, and our labor should be in vain," 1 Thessalonians 3:5. Paul's

prayer for them, "And may the Lord cause you to increase and abound in love for one another, and for all men, just as we do for you," 1 Thessalonians 3:12. This was followed by the assurance that The Lord would find their hearts "unblameable in holiness before our God and Father," 1 Thessalonians 3:13.

I don't know about you, but I want to be found blameless in holiness before God. A way to ensure this is to follow Paul's instruction to increase and abound in love for one another. Of course, this goes against extreme sentiments in the world today, but I want to follow God's words, not man's.

REFLECTION

1. Do you know someone who models abounding love for you? Who and how?

2. To whom can you demonstrate abounding love? What is your plan to do so?

3. Turn off all electronics for a bit and spend time soaking up God's abounding love for you!

DAY 24

BE READY

"And may the Lord direct your hearts into the love of God and into the steadfastness of Christ."
2 Thessalonians 3:5

Have you faced an important exam; tackled a workday; or headed up a meeting?

Have you walked in unprepared? Being unprepared causes anxiety and fear. Walking in prepared and keeping your "lamps alight" keeps fear at bay.

I was an elementary school teacher. It became quickly evident to me any day I walked into the classroom unprepared guaranteed a day that would not run smoothly. Whether they were 5 or 12 years old, students sensed when I was not prepared. Conversely, a well-planned week flowed smoothly, no matter what changes the day brought.

Luke warned, "Be dressed in readiness, and keep your lamps alight," Luke 12:35. The apostle Paul, in 2 Thessalonians 3:5, recounts, "And may the Lord direct your hearts into the love of God and into the steadfastness of Christ.",

Jesus compared us to a servant awaiting the master when He told us to be eternally ready and keep our lamps alight. Similarly, Paul  advised keeping our hearts directed toward God's love. Both Luke and Paul remind us to direct our hearts to the One who loves us.

Jesus was reminding us He loves us and wants us to be prepared for His return. As preparing for an exam, meeting, or a day of teaching, being prepared for Jesus makes every day a pleasure. We can walk through our day knowing we are ready to meet the One who loves us!!!

REFLECTION

1. How are you preparing for Jesus' return?

2. Are you ready? Why or why not?

3. Whom can you help prepare for the day they meet Jesus?

JOHN'S MIRACLE

MY STORY

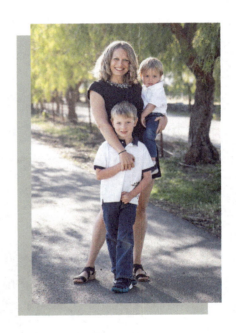

I grew up in the mid-'50s to mid-'70s in a bustling household. We were a family of nine people, the same mother and same father, and seven children. I was number two. I understand none of us were planned, but I do know that each one of us was loved unconditionally by our parents and one another. Of course, we had the usual sibling rivalries and quarrels, but I am confident each of us would be an example of *John 15:13, "Greater love has no one than this, that one lay down his life for his friends."*

Our parents have gone to their heavenly home, but all seven of us are alive and well! We live in four different states, and only manage to see each other when a niece or nephew marry or graduates. I love them all and am always happy to be together.

Much like a parent, which I sometimes was to my younger siblings, I have a special place in my heart for each of my brothers and sisters. John is the middle child of this large family. John enlisted in the U. S. Navy at 18 and loyally served our country. Shortly after discharge, he joined a group of friends on an adventure looking for gold in the mountains of Idaho. During  a trip returning from town for supplies, he was a passenger in a truck that took a nasty curve, fell off the side of the road, and ignited into flames. The truck rolled several times down a steep embankment and came to rest among large trees in a desolate area. There was no civilization for miles.

The next part of this story is an example of a true miracle. The truck was in flames, and John could not get out because the door was welded shut (it was an old truck). However, some backpackers just happened to be right there and saw the entire accident. They pulled John out through the window and called for help. He was airlifted to Salt Lake City, Utah, to the burn center at the University hospital.

John had 3rd-degree burns over 30% of his body, but with good care and much work, he is alive and thriving. He has a son and daughter, and three beautiful grandchildren.

I believe God sent those hikers to the right place at the right time to save John's life.

John is the guy who brings gift cards to give to a flight attendant who is kind to others. He is the guy who opens the door for people and has a kind word for everyone. John is a walking miracle, and he tries to share that with the world.

We are told in Jeremiah 29:11, *"For I know the plans that I have for you, declares the Lord, plans for welfare and not for calamity to give you a future and a hope."* I am thankful God showed my family His love for John, and us, by sending his "angels" to rescue my brother. This is a pure example of God-loving. He has plans for John's life. He has plans for John's children, and grandchildren, and their heirs.

"For the Lord loves justice, and does not forsake His godly ones." Psalm 37:28

Maureen

DAY 25

SPIRIT WITHIN

"For God has not given us a spirit of timidity, but of power and love and discipline."
2 Timothy 1:7

A postle Paul, nearing the end of his earthly ministry, felt compelled to write Timothy to remind him of critical information.

First, he reminded Timothy, he had received *"the gift of God which is in you" 2 Timothy 1:6.* It was this gift Timothy was destined to share the Good News with everyone. *2 Timothy 1:7* describes our gifts, *"For God has not given us a spirit of timidity, but of power and love and discipline."* These, my friend, are true gifts! Not only were these given to Timothy, but to every true disciple of the Lord Jesus Christ!

The opposite of "timidity" is "boldness." We are to be bold when sharing about Jesus. We are not to fear the trials of this world because we have been given a spirit of power—the power to overcome.

This verse assures us we have been given the spirit of **love**. I believe this means we can give **love**, receive **love,** and share **love**. This means we can even **love** those who may seem unlovable.

The final gift in this verse is the spirit of discipline. Self-discipline is tough for me. I require self-discipline to deny myself sugary treats or to stay still long enough to write. 2 Timothy 1:7 has long been one of my "go-to" verses as it reminds me I have the spirit of self-discipline.

The world may seem scary and mean and out of control. We need not worry. The Spirit to conquer all these things was a gift from God and lives inside us.

REFLECTION

1. When have you boldly reached out with the good news of Jesus? If you haven't yet done so, make a plan and follow through.

2. When has the spirit of love reached inside you to let you know the King loves you?

3. I challenge you to memorize this verse for the next time you need the willpower to resist temptation.

DAY 26
GOD FIRST LOVED US

"We know love by this, that He laid down His life for us; and we ought to lay down our lives for the brethren."
1 John 3:16

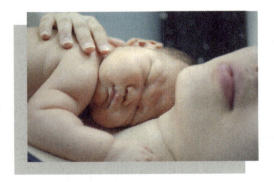

This verse is not to be mistaken for John 3:16 about agápé love, the unconditional love of God.

This verse, 1 John 3:16, "We know love by this, that He laid down His life for us; and we ought to lay down our lives for the brethren," cites God's agápé love for us, but also expresses the type of love for one human to another in an empathy bond. Greeks call this storge love.

A similar verse is Romans 12:10, "Be devoted to one another in brotherly love; give preference to one another in honor." I recently spoke with a Marine veteran who had served in the Viet Nam war. He told me of the horrors of war not usually openly admitted and of coming home from war to be shunned in dishonor by opponents of the war. I recently heard a podcast featuring a former Navy Seal. He spoke of, "just doing his job" of putting his country and comrades before himself. He told of losing fellow Seals in battle and the sacrifices they make to uphold the Constitution of The United States and to keep us safe.

My grandson, Dustin, is serving in the United States Army. He has committed his life to living away from family and  being deployed to unknown and desolate places. Following orders to fulfill missions, he is a perfect example of these verses.

Friend, God did not give these Bible verses merely for the military or those in law enforcement. They are for every single one of us to believe, embrace and follow. We are to be devoted to and honor one another. Can you imagine a world in which everyone wants to "out-honor" the other, honoring others more than they honor you?

REFLECTION

1. Whom do you have the most difficulty honoring?

2. How will you honor that person today?

3. Cite examples of brotherly love and honor you have witnessed.

LOVING LIKE JESUS

MY STORY

It's been said there is no more incredible pain than the loss of a child. While I can agree with the statement, there is no way I can comprehend or understand it. Recently, a high school classmate of mine, April, tragically lost her son. My heart broke for her and her family. Yet even in  her grief and pain, her love and concern for others were displayed to the world.

We are taught, "We know love by this, that He (Jesus) laid down His life for us; and we ought to lay down our lives for the brethren" (1 John 3:16). Out of this heartbreak, one of a Christian's most difficult principles was witnessed by everyone watching. April's son was on life support for many days, and when

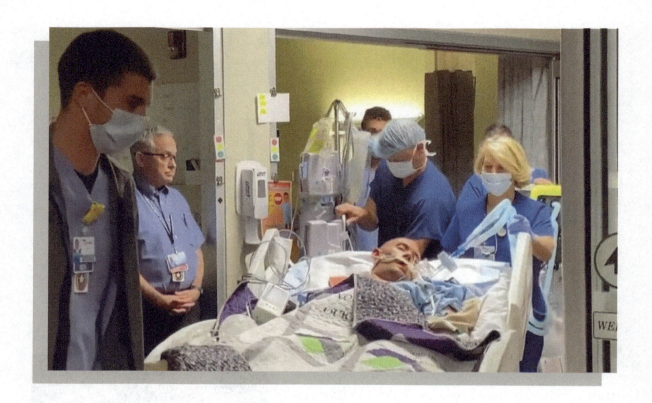

there was no hope of sustaining his life, the decision was made to donate his organs.

April turned her sorrow into someone else's joy. Despite her grief, she understood the value of life and giving life to those in need. I could never write as eloquently as she did about the event. She posted on social media the following "Somewhere tonight, a parent is praying for their child to be given an organ so they might live another day. In the next few hours, phones will begin to ring to notify people that today is the day. The day they've been hoping and praying for. The day they get another chance at life as these people make their way to the hospitals where the transplants will take place. Be in prayer. Pray for good weather, skilled pilots, a rested transplant team, and skilled surgeons.

And please pray for me. Tonight, I'm a mother who needs strength and peace as I say goodbye to my son. May his death provide many others with life."

In today's world, we want to believe loving someone should be easy, but Christ's life example and death prove otherwise. Loving as Jesus loves can be challenging, difficult, and very painful but worth the effort. I pray you never have to experience the loss April did, but I also pray this opens your eyes to the depths of love God calls us to sometimes. Will you handle it with as much grace and compassion as she?

Joel David Stinnett
April 13, 1988 - August 8, 2022

DAY 27
THE LOVE OF JESUS

*"Those whom I love, I reprove and discipline;
be zealous therefore, and repent."*
Revelation 3:19

Revelation 3:19 teaches, "Those whom I love, I reprove and discipline; therefore, be zealous and repent."

John's message to the church in Laodicea is one of seven churches to which Jesus instructed him to send the book of Revelation.

Why did the Laodicean church need discipline and repentance? First, their faith was lukewarm, they were neither hot nor cold. The city received its water from two other cities. One provided water from hot springs, the other pure cold water. But, when the waters reached Laodicea, they were no longer hot or cold, but lukewarm. Jesus said He would rather the church be hot or cold.

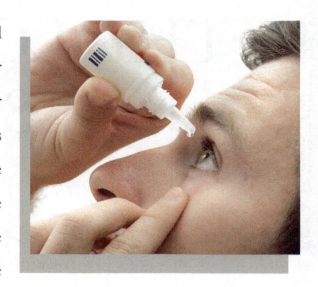

The second problem was their perception as opposed to reality. Laodicea was important for two reasons. It was a leading metropolis since it was on a major trade route. And it had become well-known for a salve that cured eye diseases developed by a local doctor. Both factors made the Laodiceans prosperous. So, they believed they were wealthy, but Jesus warned they were poor, blind, and naked. They confused their human condition with their spiritual condition.

These were Jesus' instructions to the church for healing:

1. Buy refined gold from Him to make them rich.
2. Clothe themselves with white garments to cover their nakedness.
3. Buy eye salve from Him to cure their blindness.

What did He mean? Pure gold endures almost 2,000-degree temperatures to remove impurities, making it fit for use. We, too, must have the impurities of our lives removed. White garments are an indication of a pure heart and a pure life. Finally, we are blind in many ways. We need to allow God to apply His eye salve, then we see our imperfections and sin as He does and can allow Him to work in our lives to heal us.

What was Jesus' motivation for admonishing the church? Revelation 3:19 reveals that He loves us. He loves us with agápé love, which gives us what we need, not what we want. Are you lukewarm? Do you have a perception problem? The Lord loves you enough to want you to repent.

REFLECTION

1. Whom do you have the most difficulty honoring?

2. How will you honor that person today?

3. Cite examples of brotherly love and honor you have witnessed.

DAY 28
LOVE AS THE FATHER LOVES

"Do not love (ágapó) the world nor the things in the world. If anyone loves (agápé) the world, the love (agápé) of the Father is not in him. For all that is in the world, the lust of the flesh and the lust of the eyes and the boastful pride of life, is not from the Father, but is from the world."
1 John 2:15-16

God's Word teaches, "The god of this world [Satan] has blinded the minds of the unbelieving so that they might not see the light of the gospel of the glory of Christ, who is the image of God" (2 Corinthians 4:4).

Because of Satan's schemes, the unbeliever cannot understand the light of the gospel without our Lord's intervention. Therefore, the natural state of a believer—those who love God—will conflict with the ways of the world and the "god of this world."

As believers, we walk a fine line, loving the ungodly but knowing their behavior is in direct opposition to God and His Kingdom. Each day, the Lord's return draws closer, and the more the world becomes infected with a reprobate mind and behavior.

The dilemma collides when you come face to face with the question, "How do I love the people of the world as God commands us?" "How do we become the hands and feet of Jesus to lead them to His saving grace?"

Our first weapon of love is prayer. Never underestimate the power of prayer. We must pray the Lord remove the clay from their blinded eyes, so they are capable of seeing truth. Only then will they have the opportunity to repent and turn to the only One who can save them from evil. We must also pray God

 to open doors of opportunity for us to have frank godly conversations about God's saving grace. Finally, we must be bold. We must stand and shout the goodness of God to the nations. Not only must we be the hands and feet of Jesus, but we must be His mouthpiece.*

Marta

Note: There are two different Greek words for love used in this passage. It reads as "Do not love (ágapó) the world nor the things in the world. If anyone loves (agápé) the world, the love (agápé) of the Father is not in him. For all that is in the world, the lust of the flesh and the lust of the eyes and the boastful pride of life, is not from the Father, but is from the world" (1 John 2:15-16).

REFLECTION

1. Write your prayer to God, asking for boldness, and when the opportunity arises, take a stand to speak about God's love and goodness.

2. Speak to a stranger today about how God has blessed you.

3. Who first told you about the love of Jesus? How was this accomplished?

DAY 29
ETERNAL LOVE

"And they overcame him because of the blood of the Lamb and because of the word of their testimony, and they did not love their life to death."
Revelation 12:11

This passage falls at the midpoint of the tribulation, the worst period for believers.

Though this event is yet to come, the Bible gives us abundant information to appreciate their trials and tribulations. We learn Satan and his angels will be thrown out of heaven. At that time, a voice from heaven will announce, "The accuser [Satan] of our brethren has been thrown down, who accuses them [the brethren or believers] before our God day and night" (Revelation 12:10b).

Did you notice Satan is before God, day and night, making accusations against God's own? My friend, if you believe in Jesus Christ and have made Him the Lord of your life, this is about you! Let's think about this. The accuser of the breather spends his time in the presence of God attempting to kill, steal and destroy us. We are in warfare. Life is not passive for a believer. We are warriors in an invisible spiritual realm. A warrior's life IS a walk of faith to which we have been called.

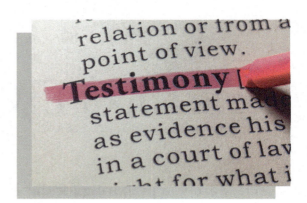

By what means does this verse say we will overcome? First, we prevail because of the blood of the Lamb. We know we are on the winning team with Jesus because His sacrificial death secured our victory. The next way we overcome is by the word of our testimony. We all have one. Some are dramatic or exciting; some are sweet, tender, and endearing. Each of us has a life that testifies to God's faithfulness. Our witness says who He is and what He has done in our lives. Lastly, disciples of Jesus Christ live boldly, without fear, since our immortal life is not here on earth but in heaven, with our Savior. We do not love (ἀγαπάω - Agapaó) our earthly life since we don't hold it in high regard. Instead, we value our promised eternity with the One who created us.

REFLECTION

1. How are you preparing for the return of Jesus?

2. What are your weapons of warfare against evil (ex: prayer, fasting, sacrifice, etc.)

3. Write your personal testimony.

Philia

φιλέω

To have love or affection for someone or something based on association.

φιλέωa: ὁ φιλῶν πατέρα ἢ μητέρα ὑπὲρ ἐμὲ οὐκ ἔστιν μου ἄξιος 'the person who loves his father or mother more than me is not worthy of me' Mt 10:37.

φιλία: ἡ φιλία τοῦ κόσμου ἔχθρα τοῦ θεοῦ ἐστιν 'affection for the world is hostility toward God' Jas 4:4. In a number of languages, it may be difficult if not impossible to speak of 'affection … is hostility.' Frequently it is necessary to relate such emotional attitudes to individuals so that this expression in Jas 4:4 may be rendered in some languages as 'people who love the things in the world are against God.'

DAY 30
AGÁPÉ VS. PHILIA

"He said to him the third time, "Simon, son of John, do you love Me?" Peter was grieved because He said to him the third time, "Do you love Me?" And he said to Him, "Lord, You know all things; You know that I love You." Jesus said to him, "Tend My sheep.""
John 21:17

To truly understand this conversation between Jesus and Peter, we must travel back to the original language.

Love has several meanings in the Greek language. Two of these meanings are used in this verse. Agápé is unconditional, sacrificial love; the other, philia, is affection for a close friend.

Let's put the conversation in context. "When they had finished breakfast, Jesus said to Simon Peter, 'Simon, son of John, do you love (agápé) Me more than these?' He (Peter) said to Him (Jesus), 'Yes, Lord; You know that I love (philia) You.' He said to him, 'Tend My lambs.' He said to him again a second time, 'Simon, son of John, do you love (agápé) Me?' He said to Him, 'Yes, Lord; You know that I love (philia) You.' He said to him, 'Shepherd My sheep.' He said to him the third time, 'Simon, son of John, do you love (agápé) Me?' Peter was grieved because He said to him the third time, 'Do you love (agápé) Me?' And he said to Him, 'Lord, You know all things; You know that I love (philia) You.' Jesus said to him, 'Tend My sheep'" (John 21:15-17). Every time Jesus used the word agápé, Peter used the word philia.

Earlier, Peter had egregiously denied Jesus three times. Peter had already denied Jesus three times. If I were Peter, I would have gone from a confidant disciple who boldly claimed, "Even though all may fall away because of You, I will never fall away" (Matthew 26:33) to a meek and remorseful disciple. Feelings of guilt and failure would creep into my mind. We can't know Peter's thoughts, but it's reasonable to conclude that since that failure, Peter didn't trust himself capable of unconditionally loving Jesus or His people.

Jesus knew Peter would one day revert to being the bold, outspoken leader and become a wise and vigilant servant of the Lord. One day Peter would be martyred on a cross just like his Savior. You may be a meek, remorseful disciple, but Jesus is calling you to be the wise, outspoken leader. "Trust in the Lord with all your heart, and do not lean on your own understanding. In all your ways acknowledge Him, and He will make your paths straight" (Proverbs 3:5-6).

REFLECTION

1. Describe a time when you denied Jesus to fit in with the crowd.

2. How did you feel afterward?

3. How have you demonstrated your trust in the Lord?

YOUR STORY

We want to know what God has done in your life!

Write your testimony here or send an e-mail to **info@wogt.org**.

If this Devotional ministered to you, please leave us a review of where you purchased the book and recommend it to you friends and family.

Follow us on our Social Media:
- Words of Grace & Truth
- WordsOfGraceandTruth
- Marta Greenman
  Maureen Maldonado
- MartaEGreenman@WordsGraceTruth
- MartaEGreenman

Contact us:
Words of Grace & Truth
PO Box 860223
Plano, TX 75086

info@wogt.org
469-854-3574

Made in the USA
Las Vegas, NV
24 February 2024